Tiny the Tree Frog
Tours Bermuda

Illustrated and written by
Elizabeth A. Mulderig

Edited by Tuppy Cooper
Designed by David Conrad

Published by
The Bermudian Publishing Company Limited
P.O. Box HM 283
Hamilton HM AX
Bermuda

Printed in Singapore

First Edition December 1992
Reprinted March 1994

ISBN 976-8104-24-4

The **Tree Frog** *(Eleutherodatylus johnstonei)* is among the most well-known features of Bermuda nightlife. As the sun sets and dampness falls, the tree frog's high-pitched 'gleep' begins to fill the night air. The sound is a result of the frogs talking to each other from high in a tree or under a garden rock. Although the frog is not indigenous to Bermuda, it has become a 'native' as it would not be a true Bermuda night without its distinctive sound. Most tree frogs sleep through the day. Most, that is, except Tiny…

To my parents with love

Special thanks to Patricia, Mandy, Leah, David, Kevin and Tuppy.

Tiny the tree frog
decided one day
to discover Bermuda
in his own special way.

Plucking his courage
and stifling a yawn,
Tiny let his playmates
snooze quietly on.

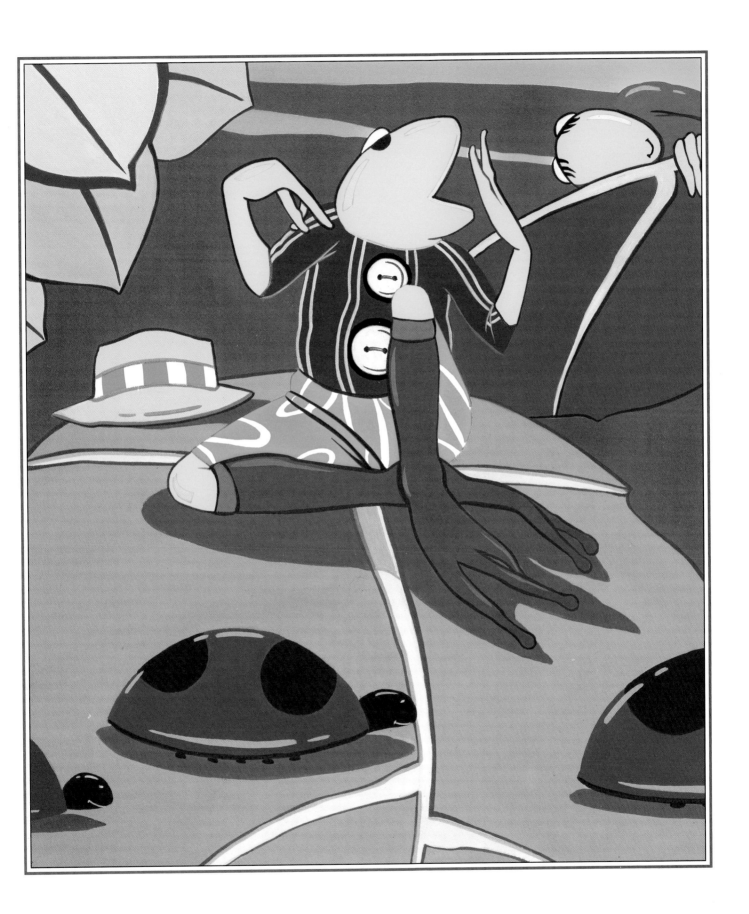

A horse and buggy
came up alongside,
he took a lollaping leap
and hopped on for a ride.

The very first stop
was an ancient stone fort,
with dungeons (no dragons)
and an old ship in port.

While next came a church
from ages ago
– steps far too steep
for Tiny's tip toe.

The perfume factory
was part of the tour,
Tiny left smelling
just like Lily du Jour.

Dark fairyland caves
were thrilling and cool,
a crystal cathedral
reflects in the pool.

Tiny stretched out
on a small pink beach,
just a weeny bit homesick
for his mates out of reach.

Eyelids were droopy,
(of course it was day)
but he staunchly continued
his adventuresome way.

Angling for turtles
in blue Devil's Hole,
'Twas the kindest of fishing
with no hook and no pole.

He heard ducks quacking
in the aquarium nearby,
the loud laugh of monkeys
and peacock's shrill cry.

Botanical Gardens
had flowers to show,
the weirdest, most wonderful
plants that can grow.

Hungry, he lingered
in town to have lunch
and relaxed in the Birdcage
to munch, munch, munch.

Off to the lighthouse
that same afternoon,
Tiny soon would be climbing
right up to the moon.

The smallest drawbridge
in the world came next,
but the ride was so bumpy
that Tiny was *vexed!*

Finally reaching
the crafts at Dockyard,
he was seat-sore and weary –
oh, touring was hard!

At long last he found
the museum of ships,
and the end of this journey
put a smile on his lips.

He gazed lonely and glum
from the pirate's black hat
'til the sun had descended
and night fell as he sat.

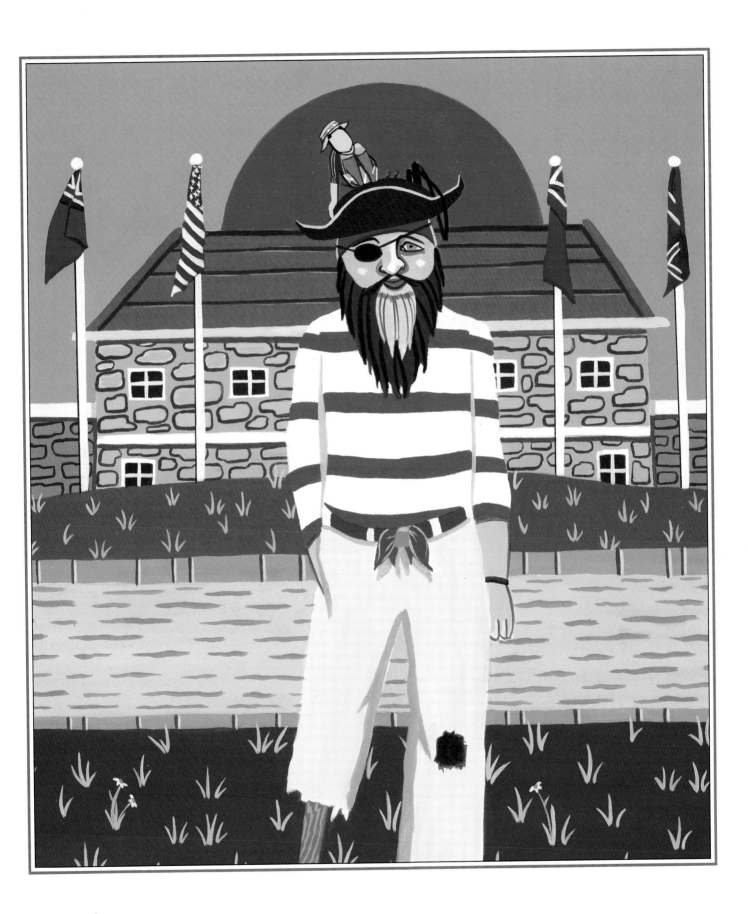

Then peeping and piping
and whistling with joy,
came trillions of tree frogs
all seeking our boy.

They clapped and clamoured
their hero to tell
of his travelling tales
and begged him as well...

To hear how Tiny
had spent the whole day
touring the Island
in his own special way.

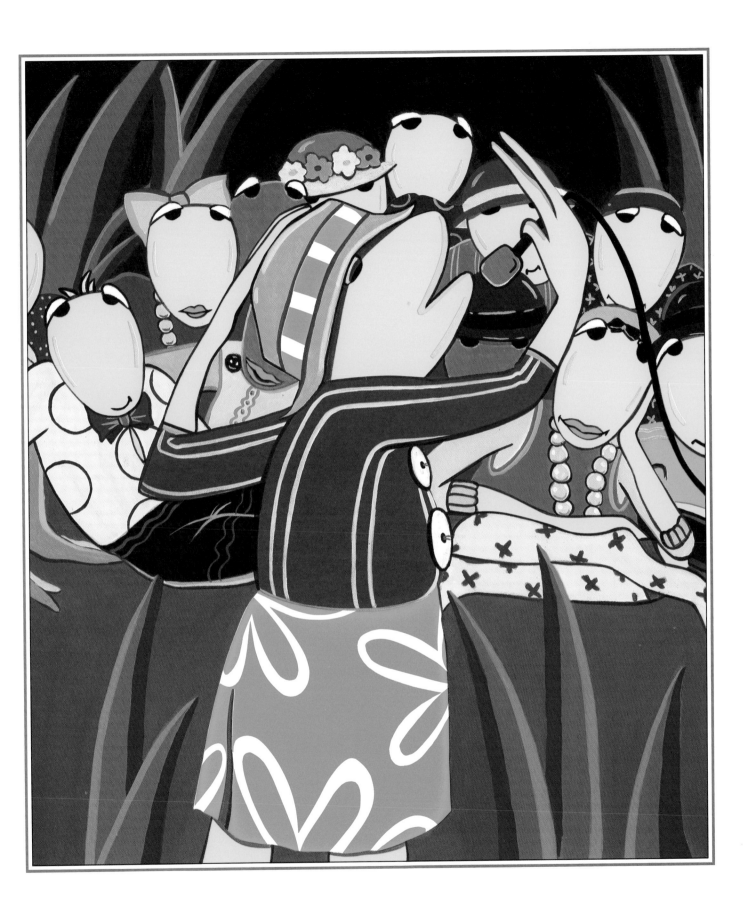

Tiny the Tree Frog
Bermuda Sights
(In order of appearance)

Bermuda Shorts
Tiny the Tree Frog is very well-dressed in Bermuda's famous fashion statement. What originated in the 1930's when women were not allowed to reveal their legs are now vital to any Bermuda wardrobe. The cool, relaxed garment is properly worn with knee socks.

Horse and Buggy
Horsedrawn carriages were Bermuda's primary means of transportation until the 1940's. This peaceful mode of travel is still a popular way to see the Island. Knowledgeable drivers relate tales of Bermuda and point out noteworthy sights.

Fort St. Catherine
One of the many remains of fortifications around the Island, Fort St. Catherine was built by the first settlers for protection against possible Spanish invaders. Now it protects replicas of the Crown Jewels and is believed to be the residence of a friendly ghost named "George."

The "Deliverance"
Survivors of the shipwrecked *Sea Venture* that led to Bermuda's eventual settlement left the Island on two small pinnaces, the *Deliverance* and *Patience*, bound for the *Sea Venture's* original destination, Jamestown, Virginia. This replica provides a factual and fascinating sight for adults and children, illustrating life on an ocean crossing in the early seventeenth century.

St. Peter's Church
This popular sight-seeing feature boasts a history dating back almost four centuries. The first settlers of the Island built their church in 1612 on the spot where this 280-year-old structure stands now. When the building was restored original "Hog Money" was found under the floor boards.

Perfume Factory
Bermuda's unique Perfume Factory is probably the most sweet-smelling property on the Island. For more than fifty years it has produced luxurious perfumes from the many flowers blooming in the surrounding gardens.

Crystal Caves
For thousands of years icicle-like formations have been growing from the ceilings in these caves eighty feet underground. Now there are pathways among the illuminated stalactites and stalagmites and bridges over crystal clear waters, fifty-five feet deep.

Pink Beaches
Tiny chips of coral from the reefs surrounding the Island are washed ashore and mixed with sand to give Bermuda's beaches their famous pink tinge.

Devil's Hole
This natural aquarium is fed by the sea through underground passageways and tempts you to try and catch green turtles with baited, hookless lines.

The Bermuda Aquarium
Twenty-eight tanks display Bermuda's ocean environment and sea life including colourful parrot fish and angel fish, black and white striped sergeant majors, sea turtles and seahorses. Outside, the aviary houses beautiful rare birds and a special treat – a "please touch" pool filled with sea urchins, star fish and sea cucumbers.

Botanical Gardens
This beautiful garden paradise offers twisting paths through hundreds of different types of flowers and plants. The "Garden for the Blind" is an aromatic treasure filled with such wonderful smells as spice trees, lemon mint, oregano and lavender.

The Birdcage
A favourite Bermuda landmark, the Birdcage was built for constables to stand in while directing traffic at the junction of two of Hamilton's busiest streets.

Gibbs Hill Lighthouse
Imagine the view of Bermuda after climbing 185 steps, 362 feet above the Island, to the top of a lighthouse that has served as a beacon for sailors for more than 150 years.

Somerset Bridge
Hailed as the world's smallest drawbridge, this bridge connecting Somerset to the mainland opens just enough to let a sailboat's mast through and is operated when passersby see a boat waiting.

Crafts Market at Dockyard
At the Royal Naval Dockyard, once an anchorage for the British Royal Navy and now transformed into a unique tourist attraction, visitors can watch Bermuda artists at work making dolls, miniature furniture, jewellery, and quilts.

Maritime Museum
Within the walls of a nineteenth century keepyard is a museum devoted to Bermuda's seafaring heritage. To get there you must cross a drawbridge over a moat and enter through an archway through the thick stone wall. Among many intriguing displays of Bermuda boats and naval artifacts is Spanish treasure retrieved from ships wrecked on the treacherous reefs that circle the Island.